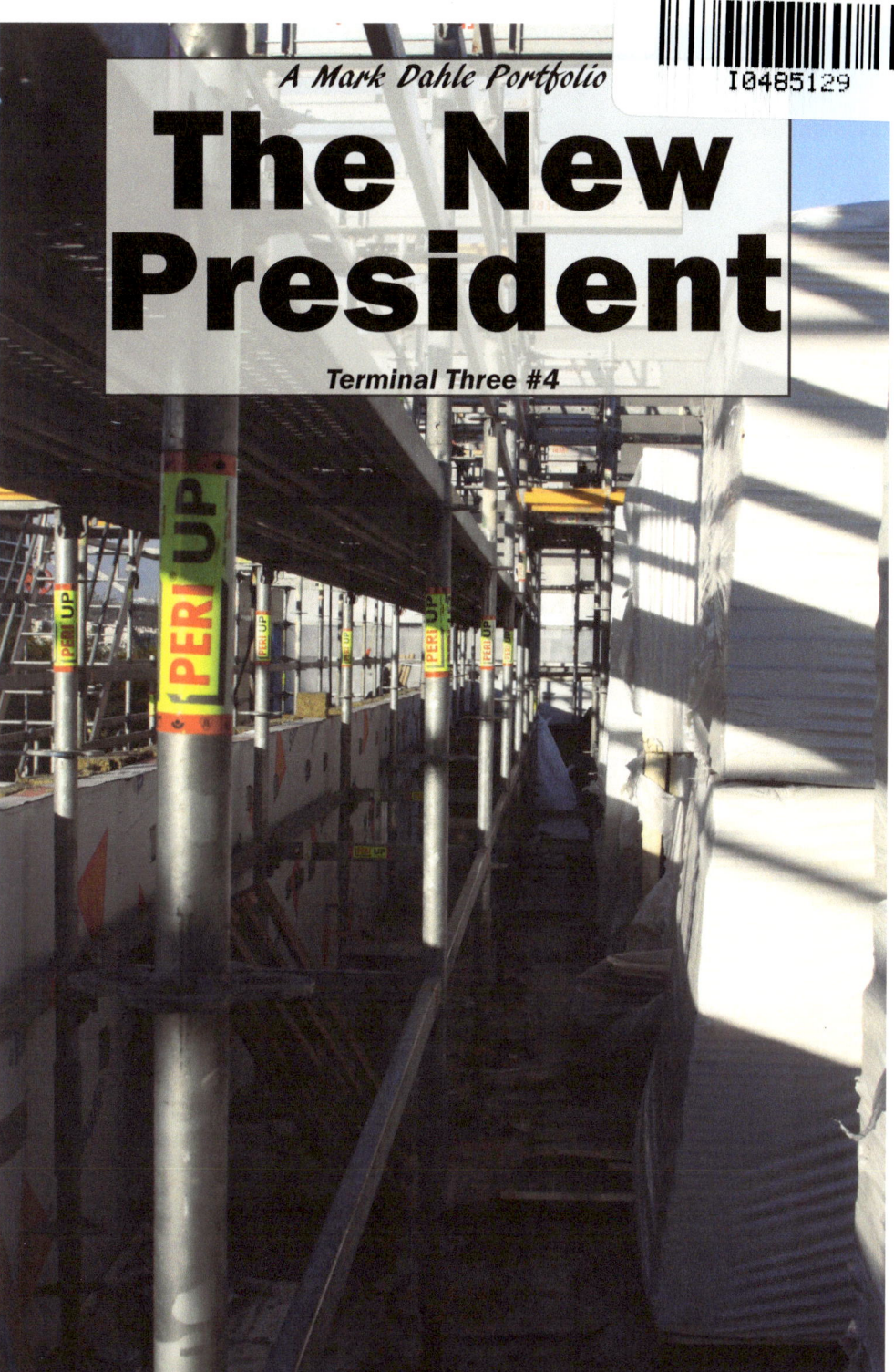

A Mark Dahle Portfolio

The New President

Terminal Three #4

Mark Dahle Portfolios can be read in a few minutes and enjoyed for a lifetime.

Unlike many picture books, the text is not related to the beautiful painting at the right and the photographs that follow. This might seem a little weird at first. One thing that helps is to order more portfolios until you get used to it. In the meantime, feel free to draw your own pictures if you like.

This portfolio includes a photo of a brilliant 36 x 24 inch painting (at the right), twenty-six beautiful pictures of Los Angeles, California, and a story about the new President of the Otto Party.

Photographs in this book are available in very limited editions. See http://www.MarkDahle.com for more information and for previews of upcoming portfolios.

We do our best to create portfolios free of editing mistakes. But it's hard to catch everything. We reward people who report errors in any Mark Dahle portfolio. For details see MarkDahle.com/Typos.html or email MarkDahle@aol.com with the subject line "Typos." Thanks!

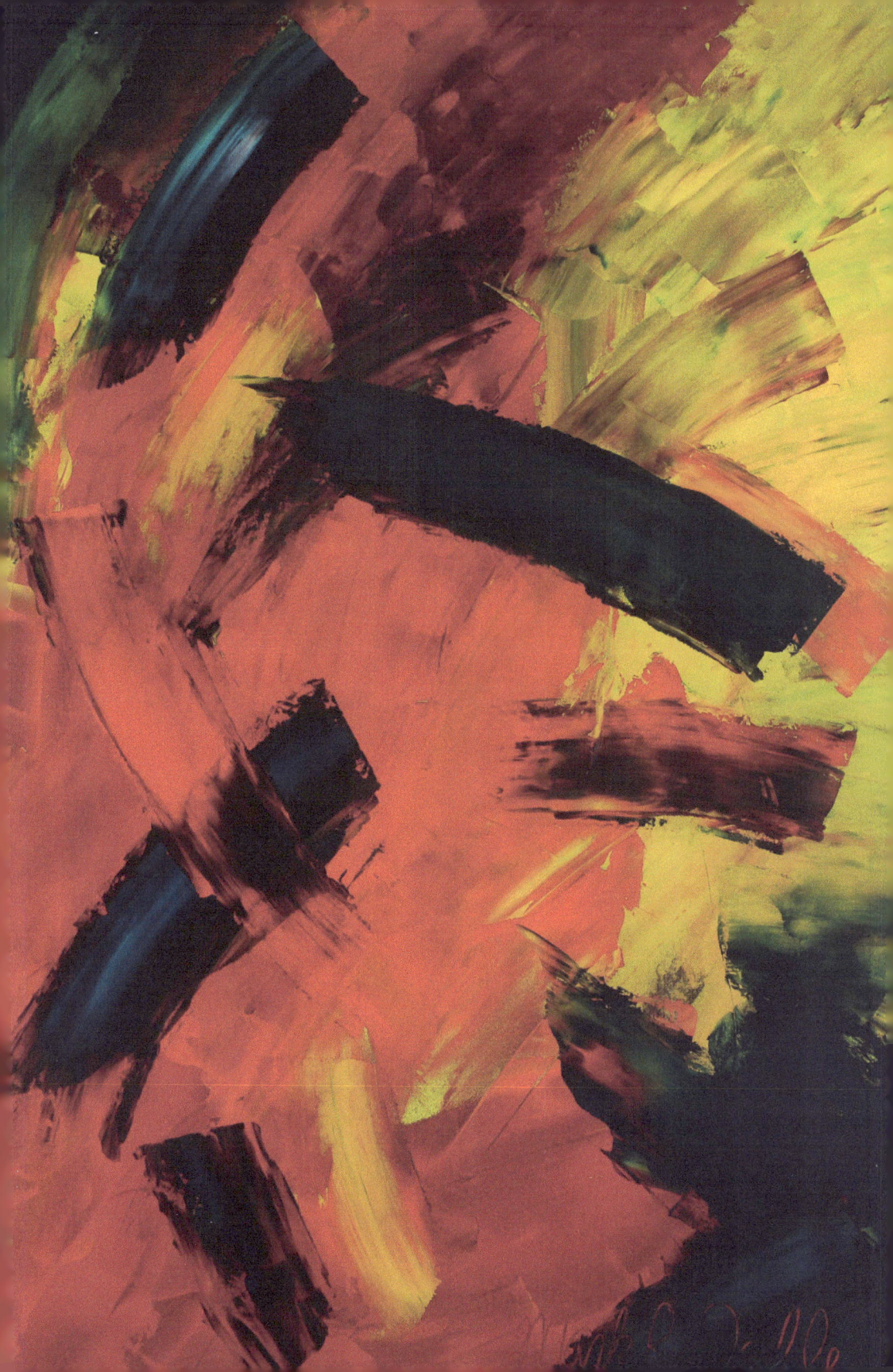

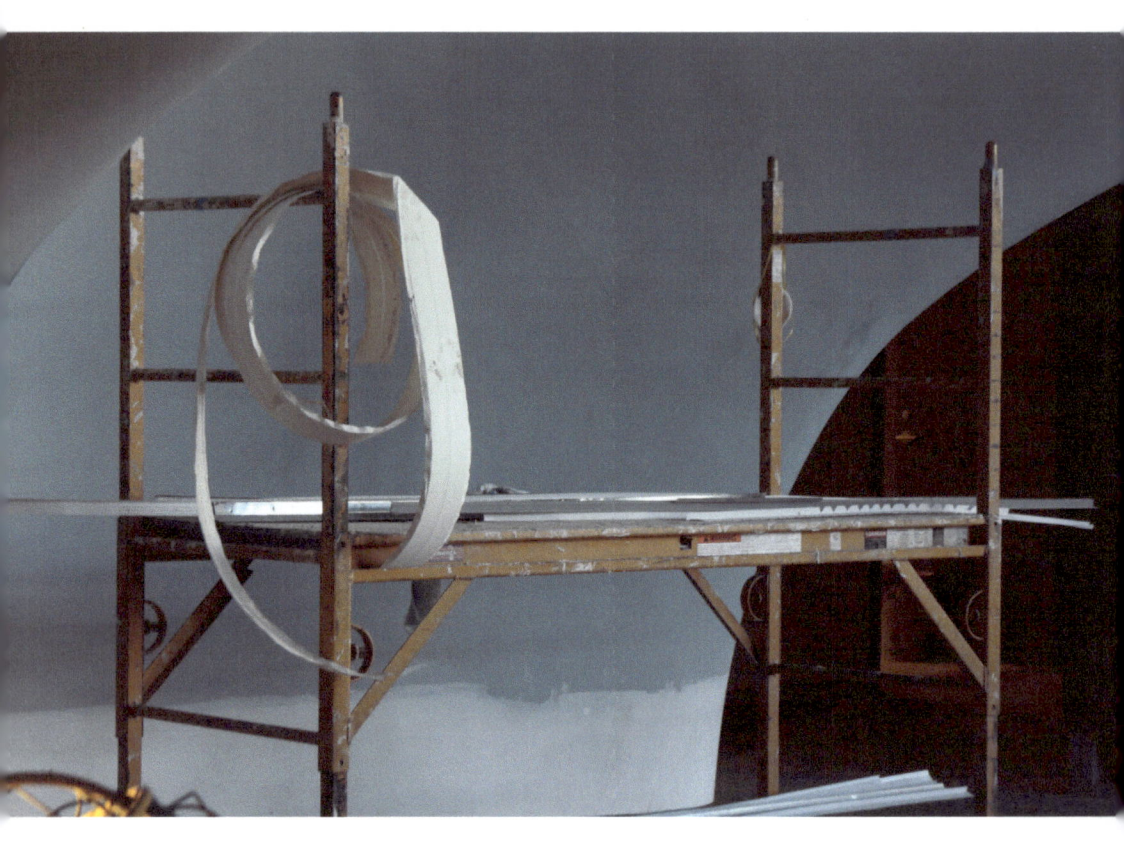

The scroll was everywhere.

An important message from the White House.
6 p.m. tonight.

Speculation throughout the world was rampant, but few guesses were as accurate as those made by members of the resistance who knew the President had likely been dead for ten days.

Leaders in the resistance had tried to estimate who was still alive in the Otto Party based on who had appeared in highlights of their convention, but there was not really enough to go on since media coverage of the convention had been so sparse. After the first three days, it stopped completely, as if the convention had ended on time.

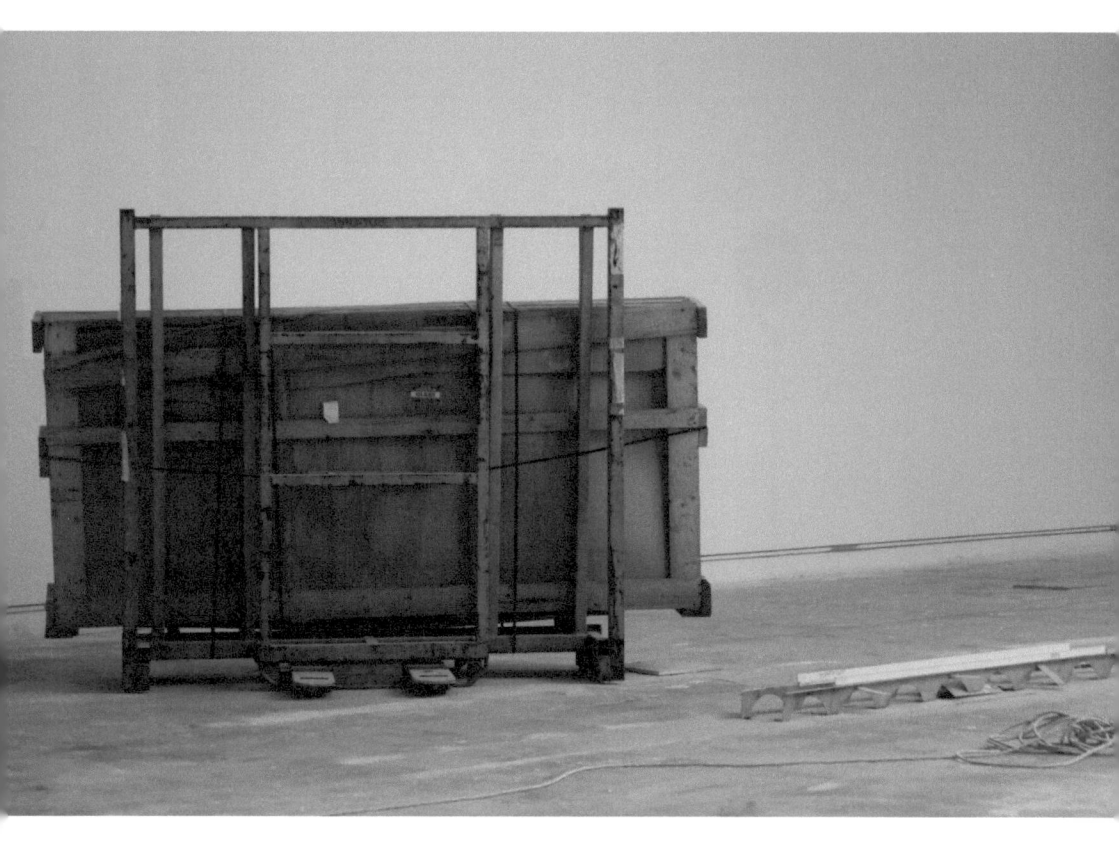

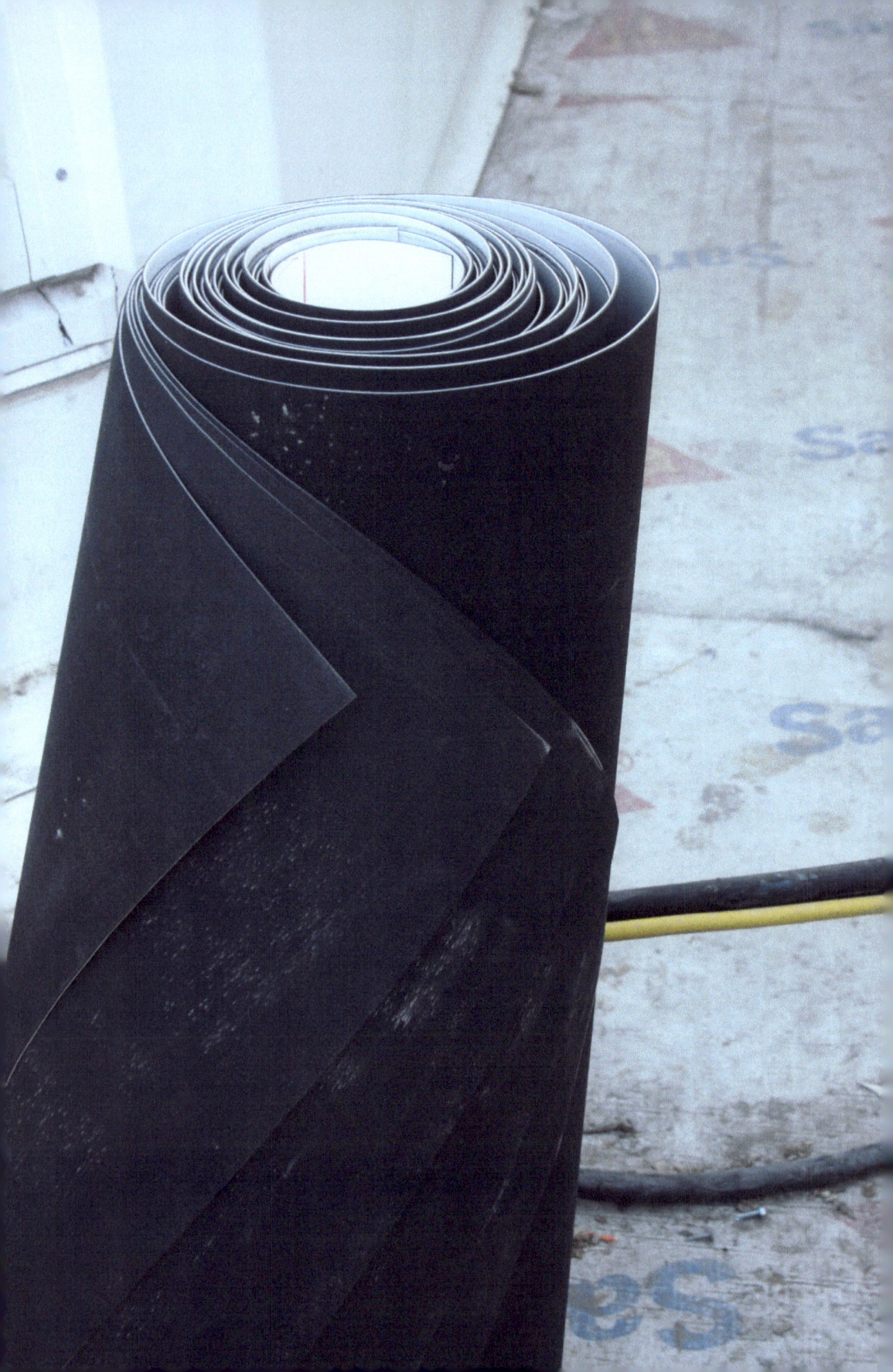

As near as people in the resistance could tell, MalPox had been confined to the area of the Whitehorse Mines so far – an extraordinary feat.

They guessed this had been possible because of the enormous restrictions already in place around the radiation site, but still it was difficult to imagine how it could have been accomplished.

For ten days the news had contained reports of a large-scale radiation leak at Whitehorse and that the area was under quarantine. Nothing more. But it looked like tonight might be the night when details about MalPox – and perhaps the President – were released.

When 6 p.m. arrived, Cooper, Jana, Han and several others were gathered around one of the underground's secure monitors – a direct feed from NewsGraph, but one that reported back no information about the watchers. More correctly, it reported back a steady stream of false information generated to give the impression that the monitor was in a normal state and was being watched by two seniors in Detroit.

At exactly 6 p.m., the announcement came, "Live from the White House, Representative Jann Smyth from South Dakota."

Jana's eyebrows went up. She had expected a leading Senator to be making the announcement.

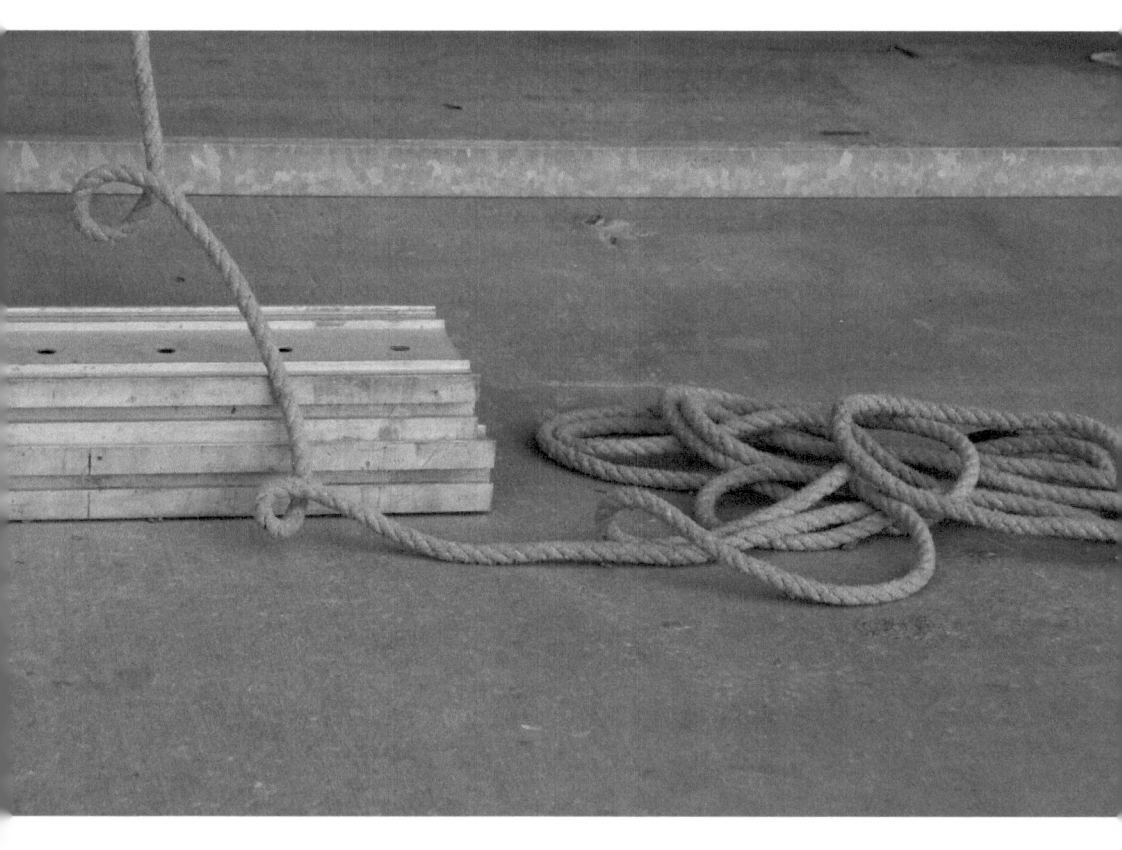

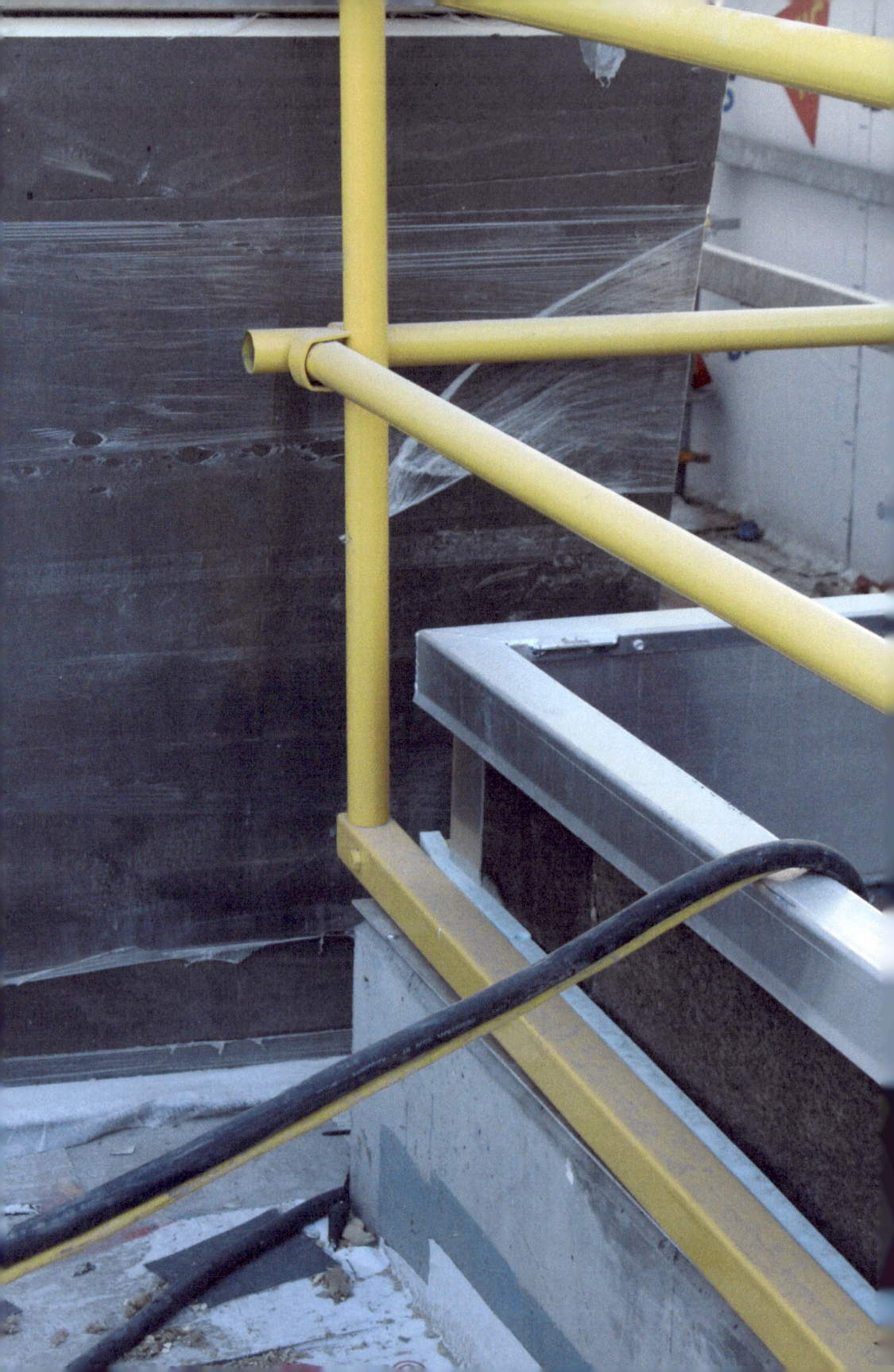

"My fellow Americans and all citizens of the world. You may not know me well. My name is Jann Smyth. I have been asked to make three announcements on behalf of the Department of Homeland Security.

"If anyone around you is not paying attention, please let them know they should not miss this broadcast."

"You with us, Han?" asked Jana. She had moved to poke him but he had jumped back. He still was recovering and even a gentle poke could be excruciating.

"Sh," he replied. "You should not miss this broadcast."

"The news I am about to give is in three parts," said Jann.

"Before we begin, I want you to know that we have not announced the news earlier to allow time to develop a solid plan. So please keep that in mind as we continue: we have a good plan for resolution of the crisis I am about to describe. You should also know that we have shut down all markets worldwide for seven days to give investors time to digest the news that will follow.

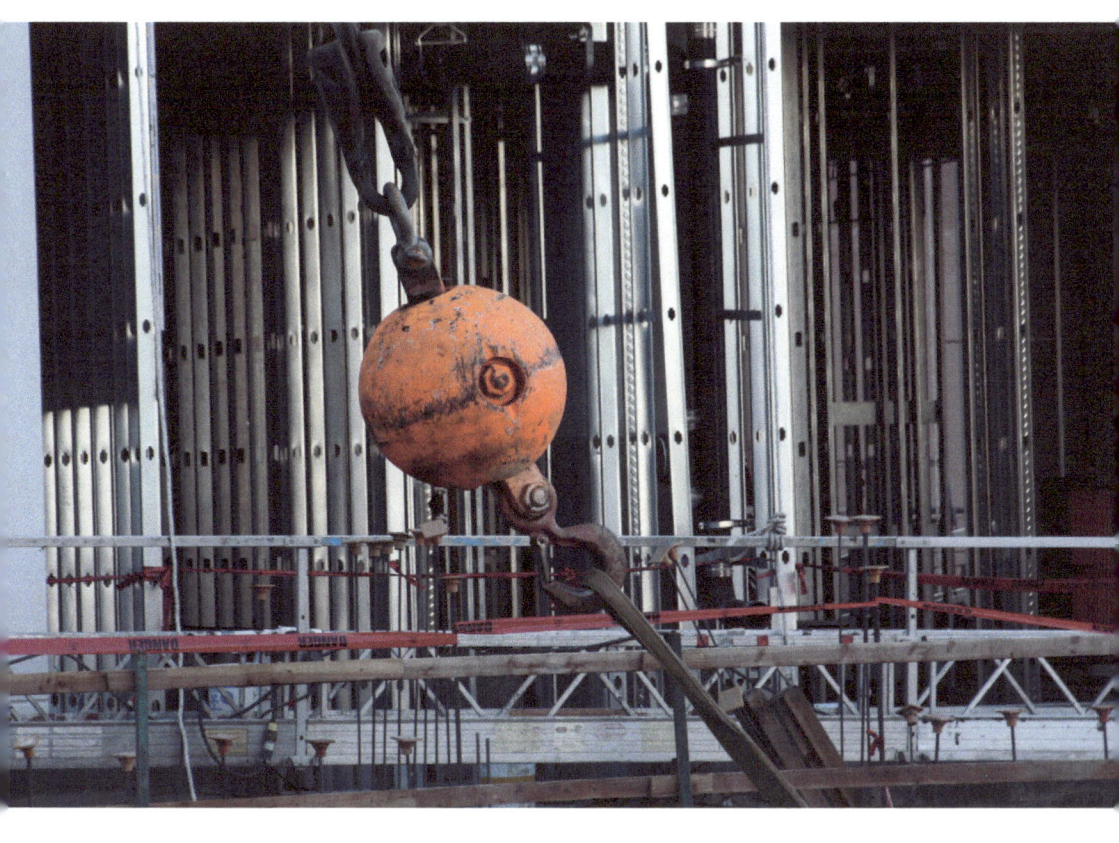

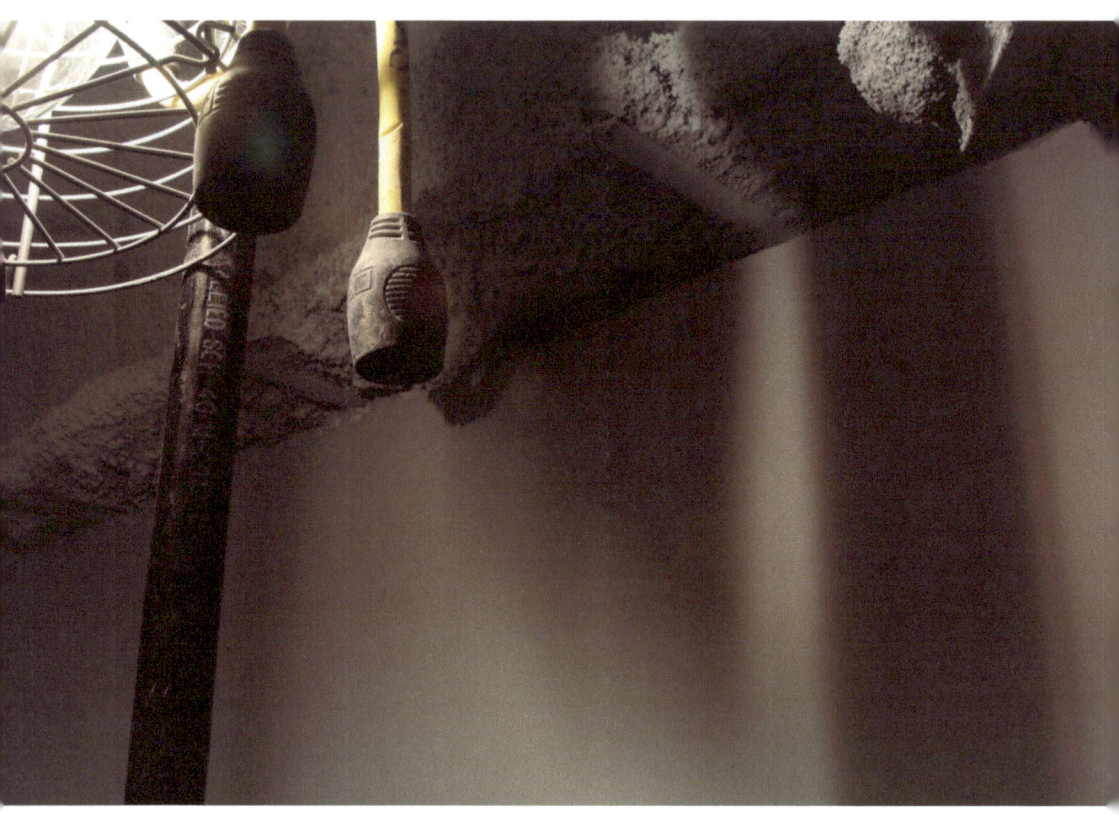

"First, reports over the last week and a half about radiation in Whitehorse have been true, but they have not been the whole story. It *is* true that there is a serious radiation leak in Whitehorse. It *is* true that Whitehorse is under quarantine. And it *is* true that no transportation in or out of the area is allowed at this time. We have blocked all exits from the area, and people attempting to escape on foot are being told to turn back. If they do not comply, they are killed. But the reason for this is not radiation.

"These extreme measures are in place because a terrorist group targeted Whitehorse and released what we believe to be three modified strains of MalPox. Almost everyone in Whitehorse is dead. We are in contact with a few survivors – perhaps as many as 100 – who seem to be immune to the virus, but whether they will survive through the length of the quarantine is unknown."

"It is a *good* thing we were able to get you out of there, Han," said Jana.

He nodded.

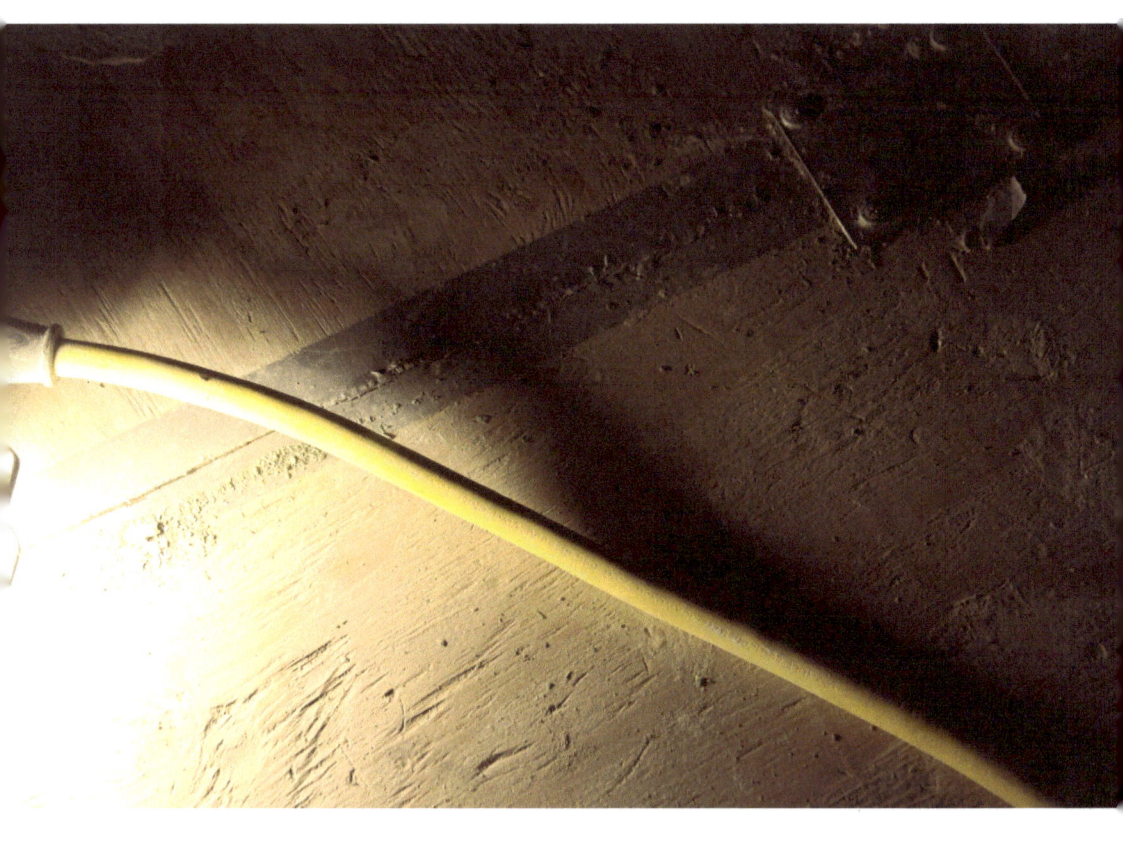

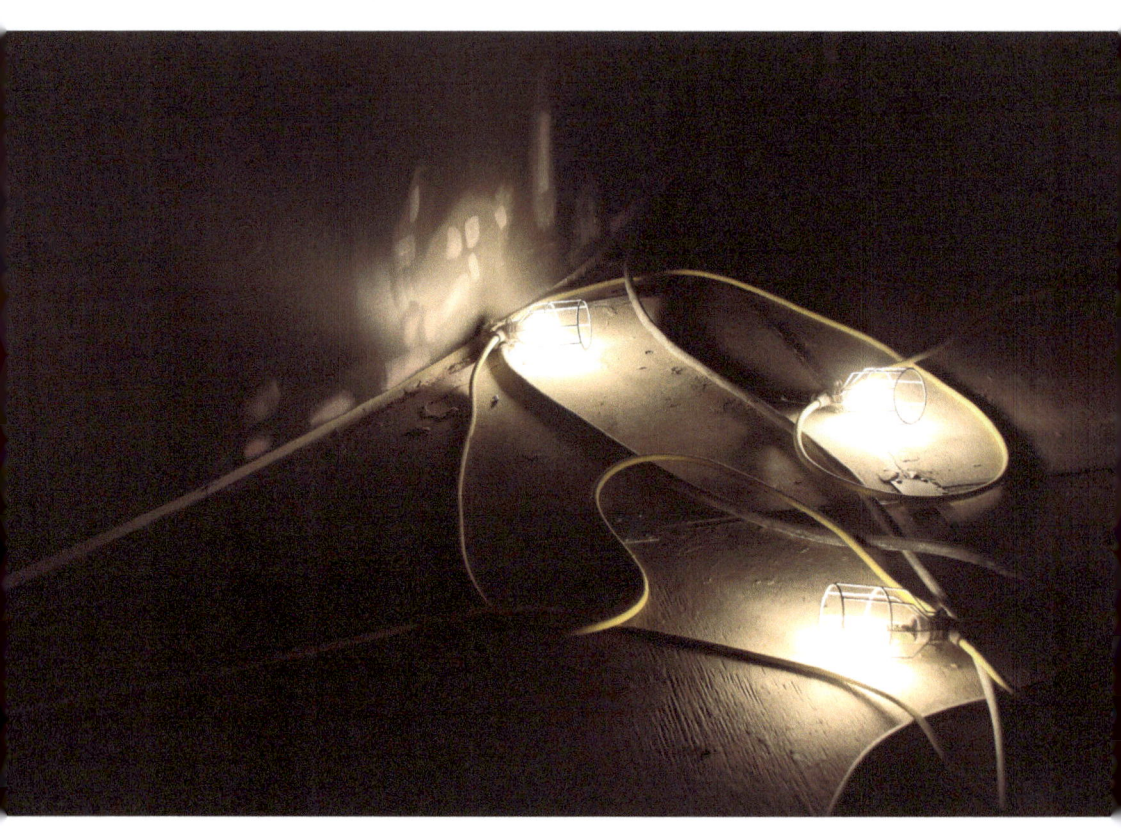

"As you know, we had attempted to confine MalPox to the moon's Quadrants A and C. With MalPox now on Earth, we will do everything we can to contain it to Whitehorse. After my comments are over, we will release information on your NewsGraph to explain how you can be safe from the virus. As you can imagine, these are perilous times. If the virus escapes the area of Whitehorse, the entire planet will be in danger. Staying informed and vigilant will be every citizen's duty in the days ahead.

"The news about MalPox is not all you need to know. There are two other pieces of news we need to discuss tonight.

"Again, I want to emphasize that a plan is in place for a secure, orderly transition through this crisis. Following my brief comments, I urge you to stay tuned to NewsGraph for updates of important things you can do.

"The second part of the news is this: because victims of MalPox die almost immediately, many of the safety features of the Whitehorse Mines were not deployed before the operators died.

"We are working with the 100 or so survivors in Whitehorse to attempt to safely shut down the automated parts of the mine. So far we have not been successful. This is difficult work; the survivors face many dangers of contamination, not just from radiation, but also from the thousands of bodies that fill the city. Most of those bodies, at least the ones that are outside, are frozen and pose no immediate danger. When spring arrives and the bodies begin decomposing, the dangers will escalate. We expect wolves, rats, flies and roaches in the area to become serious problems for the remaining survivors, and perhaps for our attempts to contain MalPox to Whitehorse. Eventually Whitehorse survivors will have trouble finding clean food and water sources. All this complicates our desire to shut down the radiation leak from the mine and to help survivors make it through this difficult season."

"Okay," said Han. "I'm liking this hospital bed more and more."

The others were silent. They hadn't considered all the problems survivors would be facing. Jana alone had seen the effects of the disease firsthand, but her exposure was in a controlled laboratory setting and not in the general population.

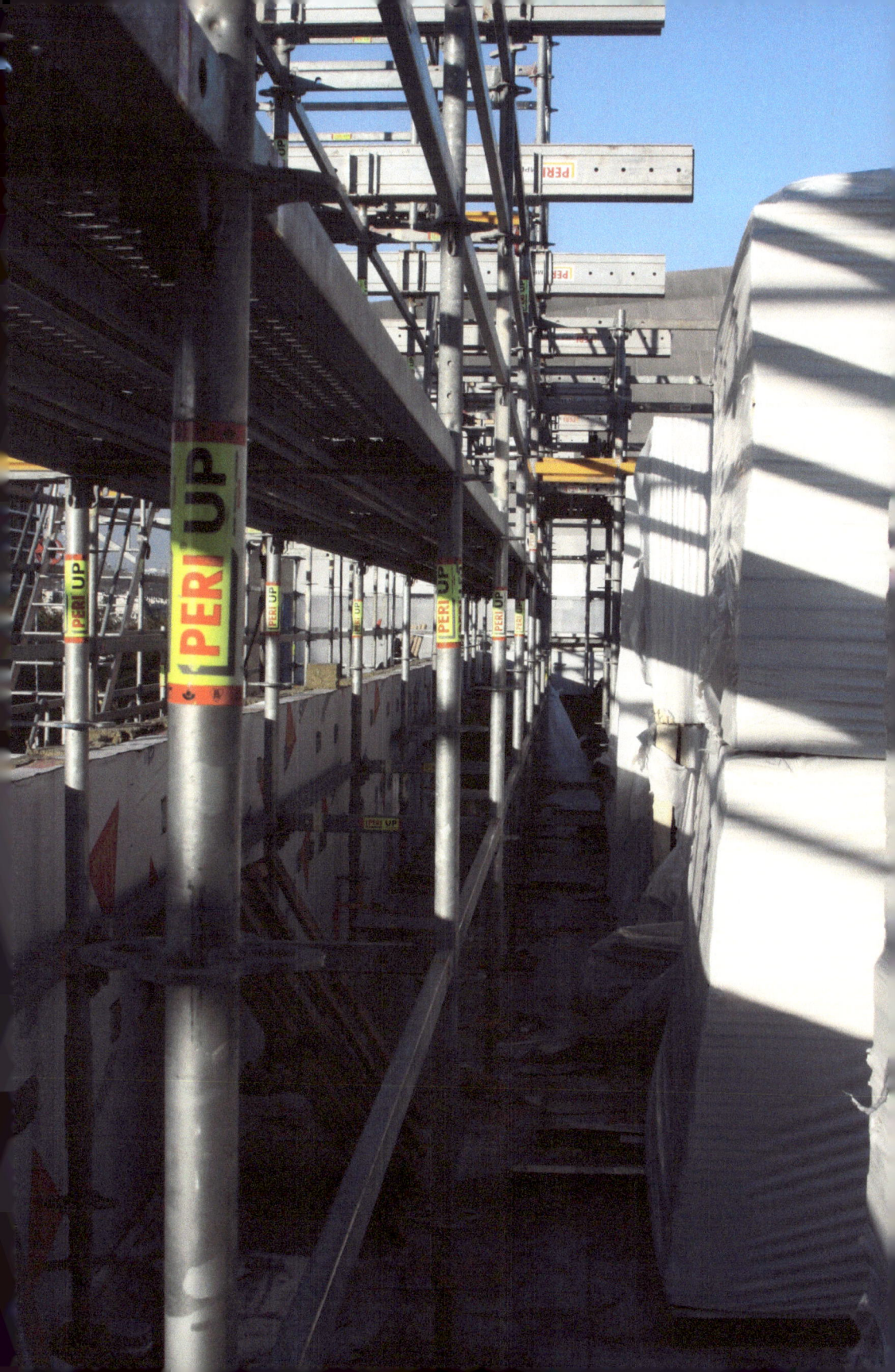

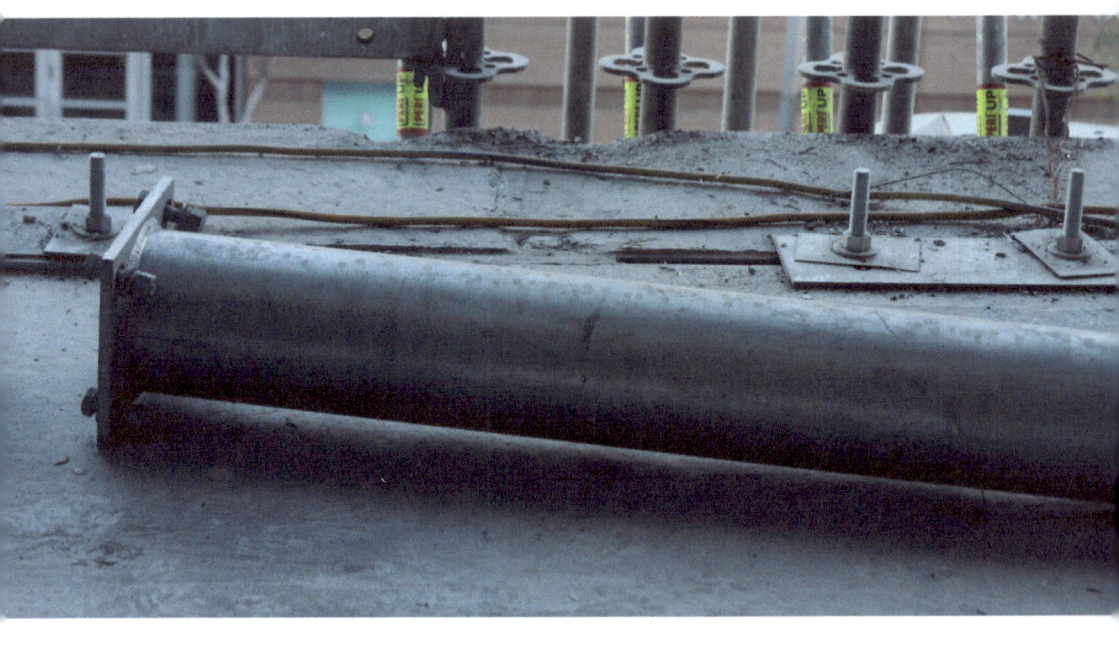

"At present," Jann continued, "the radiation danger around Whitehorse is a local event. All food, water and air has been certified as safe by the HealthCenter for anyone 1,000 miles from Whitehorse. For locations closer to Whitehorse, consult your NewsGraph.

"That's a *big* area that's not safe," said Cooper. "That leak must be *huge*."

"We now come to the third piece of news. Before I begin, I should say that for nearly two weeks your government has been drafting a plan for how to go forward in light of the unprecedented attack on our country. I appreciate the tremendous sacrifices individuals from the Otto Party and their families have made as we struggled though this and worked with a news embargo, necessary because of the sensitivity of the topics before us.

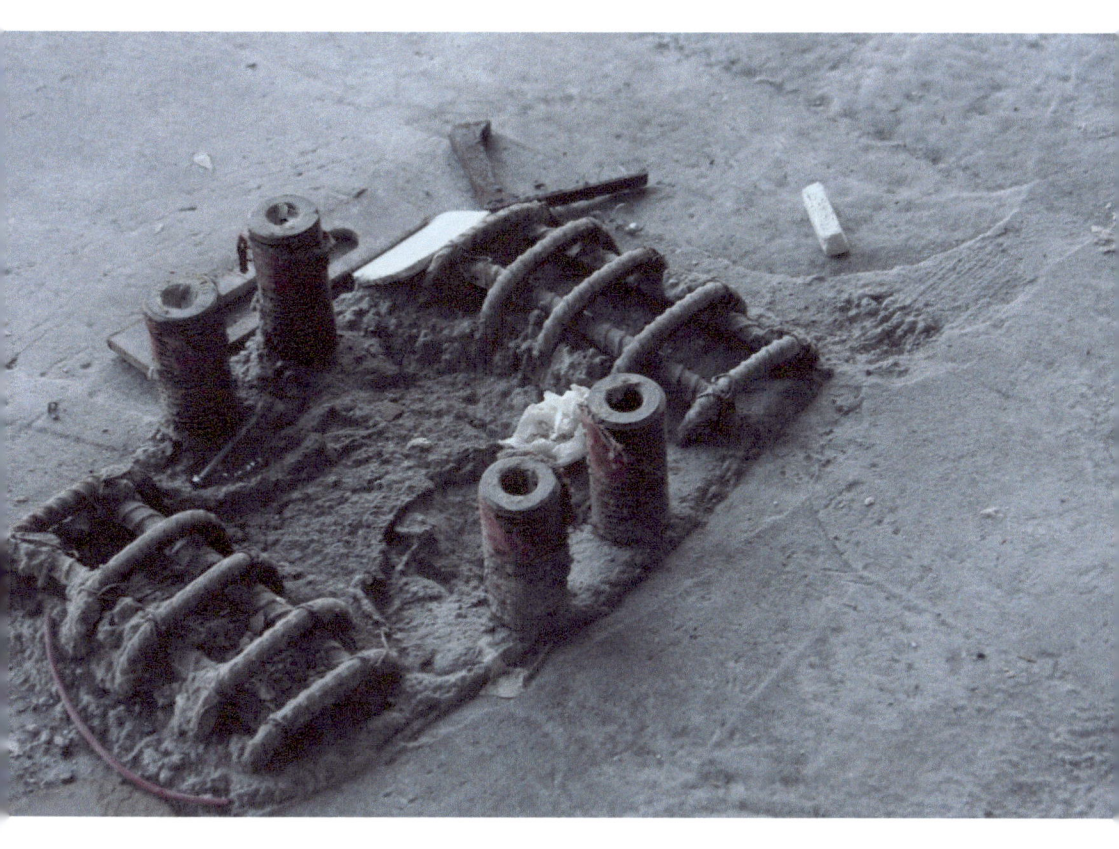

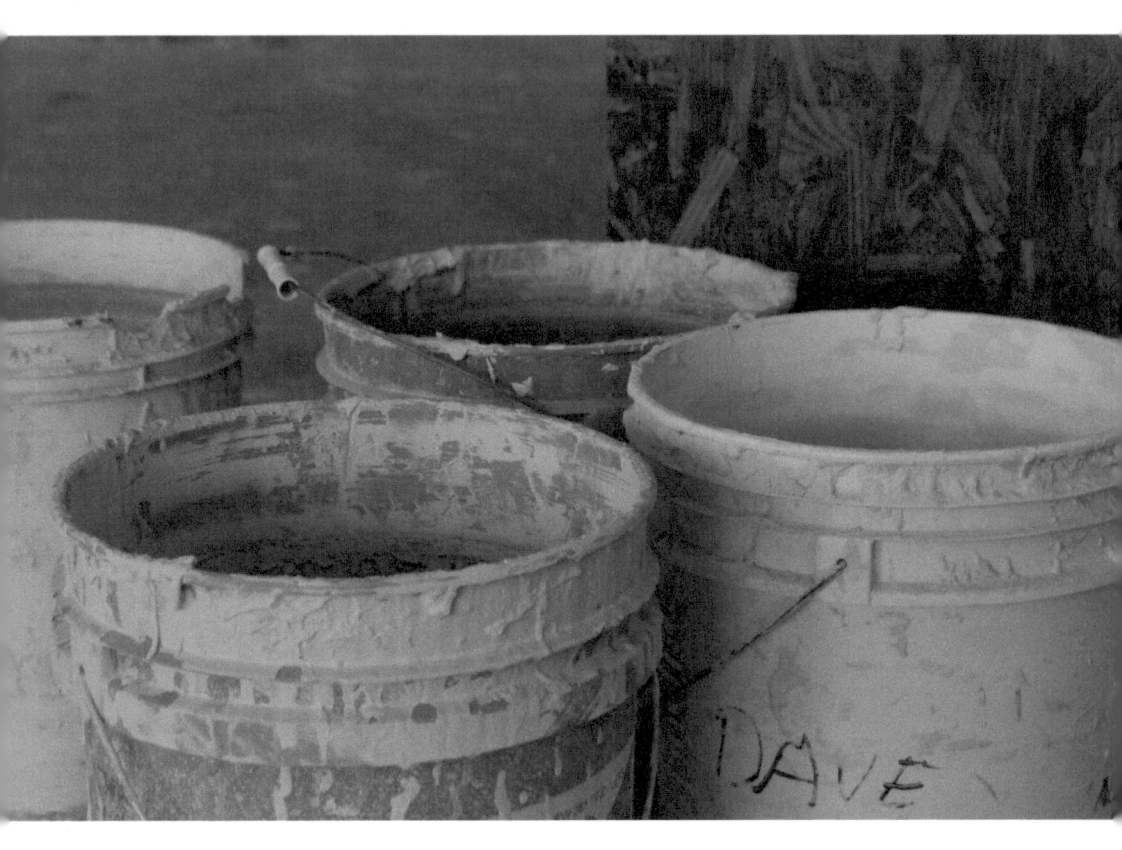

"All of us in the Otto Party, meeting in convention for the past ten days, are glad for the work that is behind us. When we came to the convention, we thought it would only last three days. Thank you to all the family members who have been so supportive during this time. We're happy to announce that tomorrow members of the party will be returning home, and we thank you and them for the service everyone has rendered to the country.

"Full details of all aspects of our recovery plan will be uploaded to NewsGraph databanks as soon as this broadcast ends so you can access particulars. But you still need to know the third piece of news.

"Our President, the cabinet, and most of the Senate were on their way to the Otto Convention a week and a half ago. Their route took them through Whitehorse at the time of the terrorist attack. We believe the attack was on them, not on the innocent people of Whitehorse or its mines.

"I regret to inform you that the President died of MalPox a minute after he was exposed. Normally this would have been announced immediately, but at the time there were no witnesses who were not also dying or compromised by MalPox. Once we discovered the tragedy, your government has been working to assess the damage, to create a working government with the leaders who are left, and to try to contain MalPox to the Whitehorse area. All the government officials passing through Whitehorse died within minutes, with one exception, Senator Fulton of Maine. Senator Fulton has survived the attack so far, but she is in extremely critical condition in quite difficult conditions. A list of officials who died will be on your NewsGraph momentarily, as will lists of who remains in office, and what their various roles are under our reorganized government.

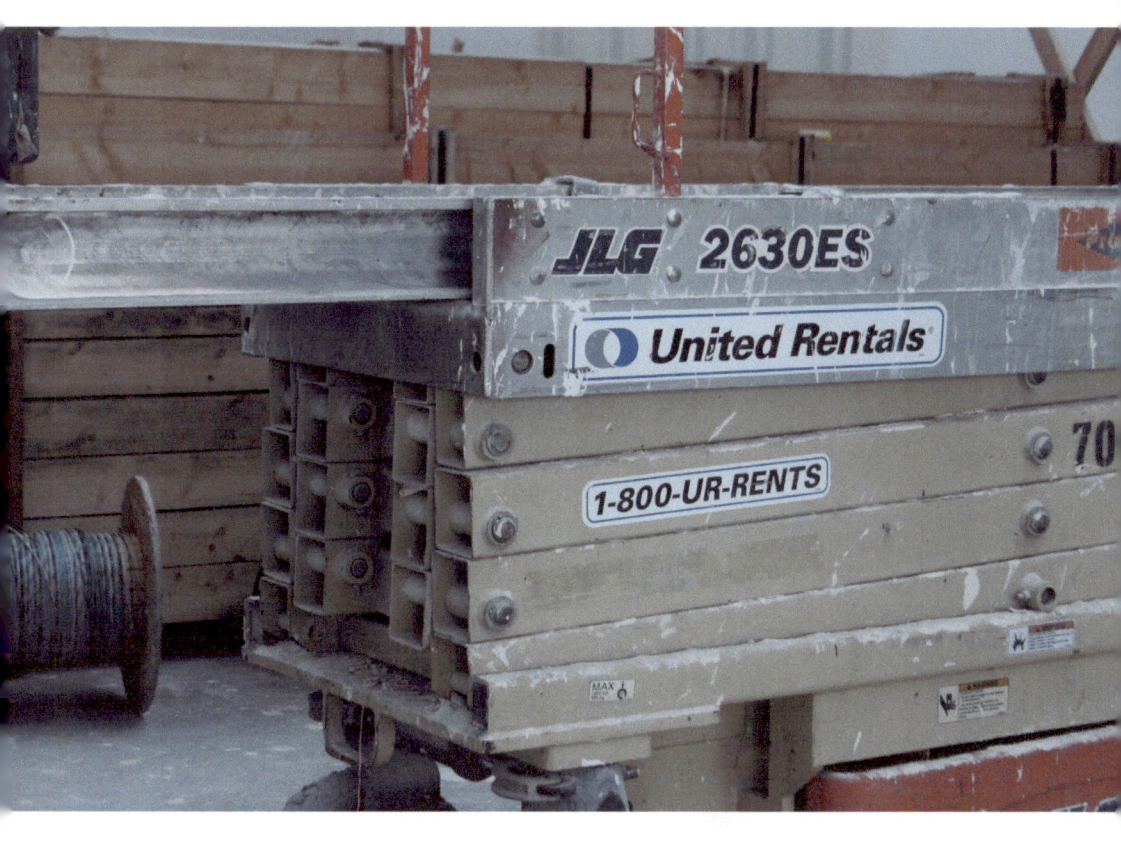

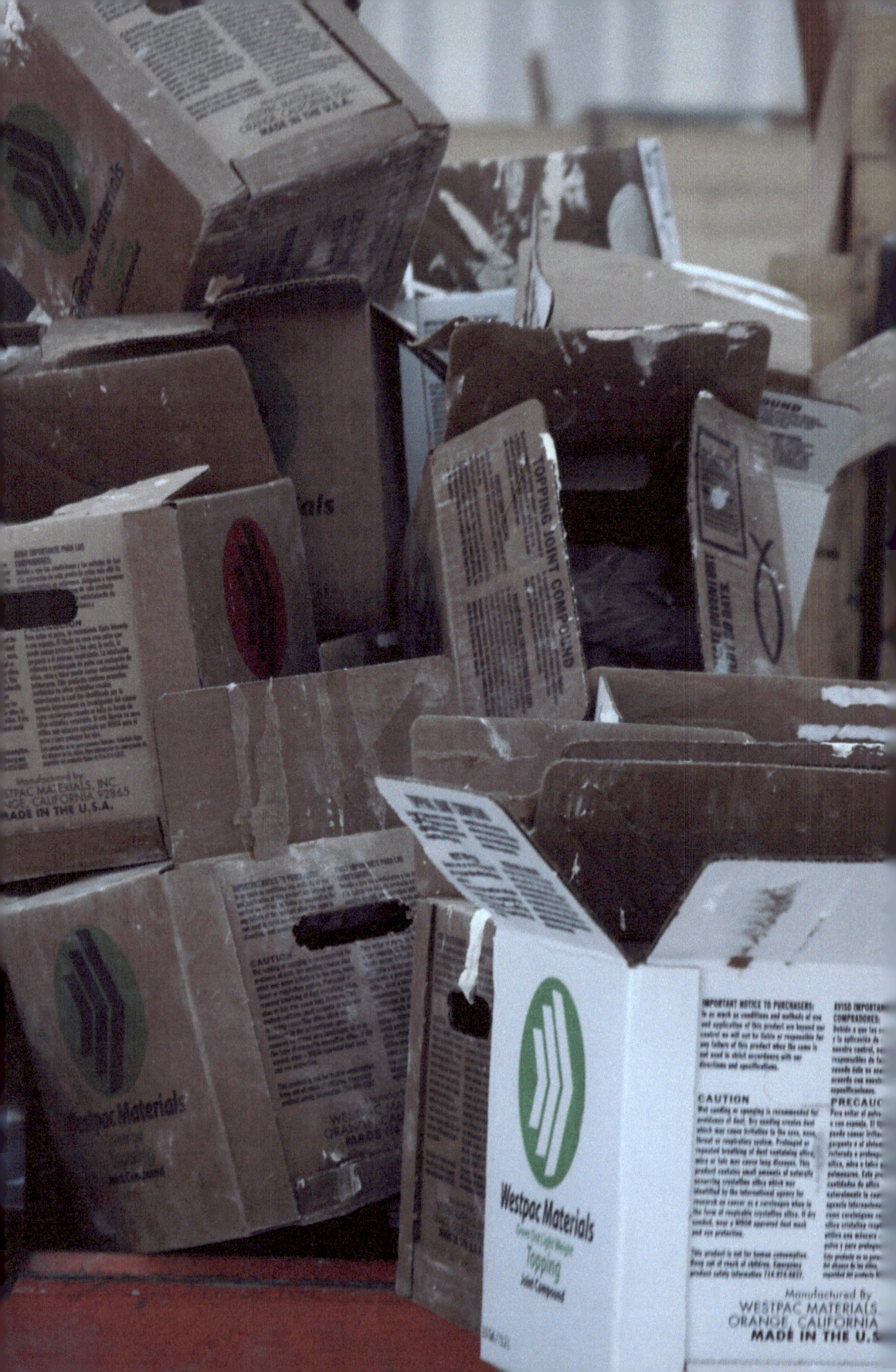

"I have been elected temporary President of the United States by the Otto Party meeting in convention. We plan to have regular elections in a year or two year for President as well as all vacated positions. In the meantime, I and the new Congress will be appointing temporary replacements for all vacated positions until the elections can be held."

Cooper grimaced. "He said most of the Senate died, plus the cabinet. That's a *lot* of replacements. No wonder it took them ten days to sort everything out."

"I realize this is a lot to process all at once," said Jann. "Your NewsGraphs will have a full databank of supplemental materials that will be available immediately after this broadcast. They will answer most of your questions.

"In good news, I can report that we have a vaccination against MalPox being prepared. All the delegates in the Otto Party are being inoculated today and tomorrow so the government will be safe from any renewed attack. Tomorrow, when Otto Party delegates have returned to Congress, the White House, and our respective homes, we will each give full localized briefings to show you much more of the plan going forward, how it affects your area, and to answer any questions you have. The vaccinations I have mentioned will be available to all, and your appointment with your AutoDoc will appear in your NewsGraph tomorrow morning. Obviously, distribution of these vaccines will take some time, but our labs are working around the clock to make sure there is enough for all in a timely manner.

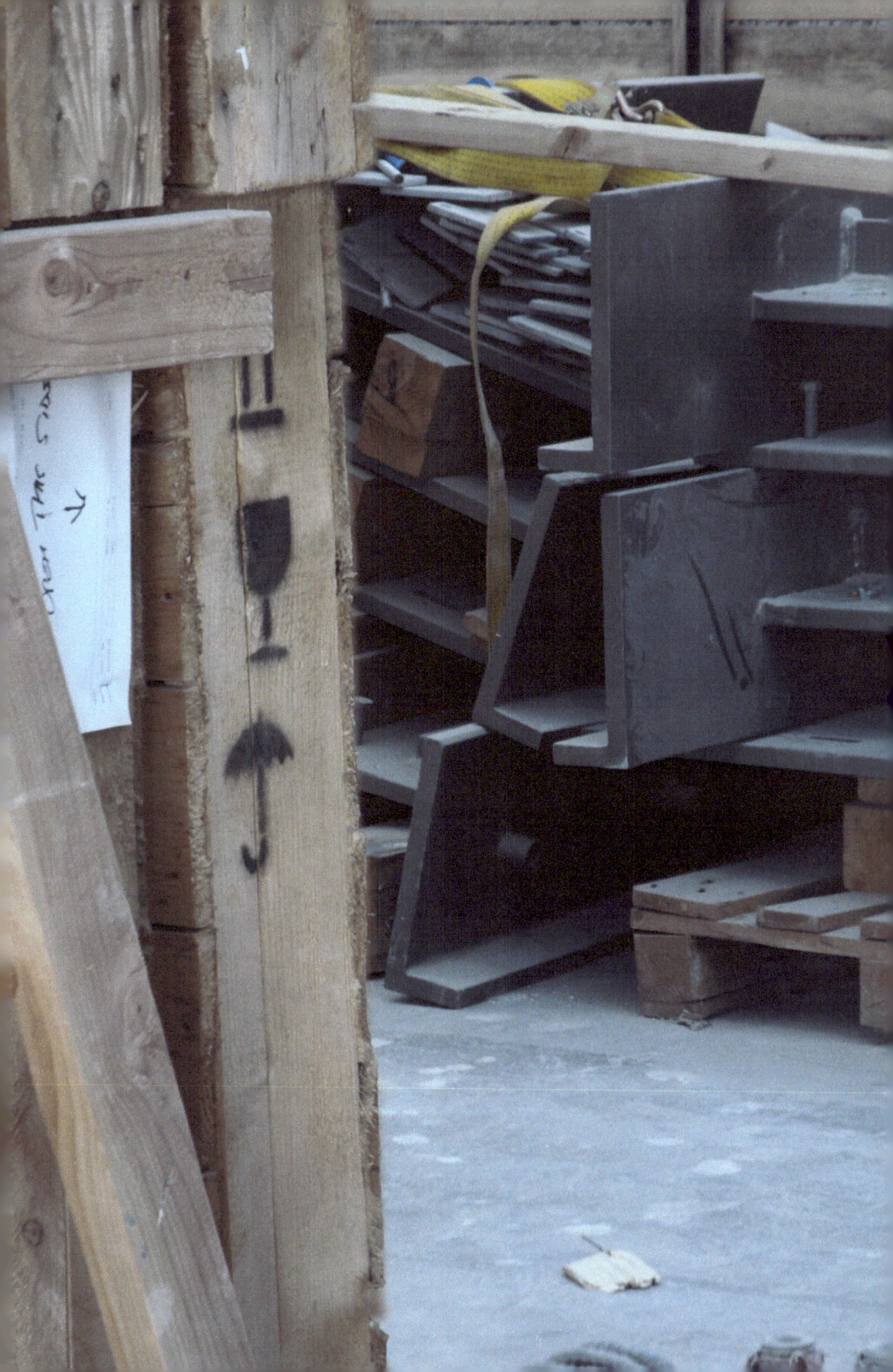

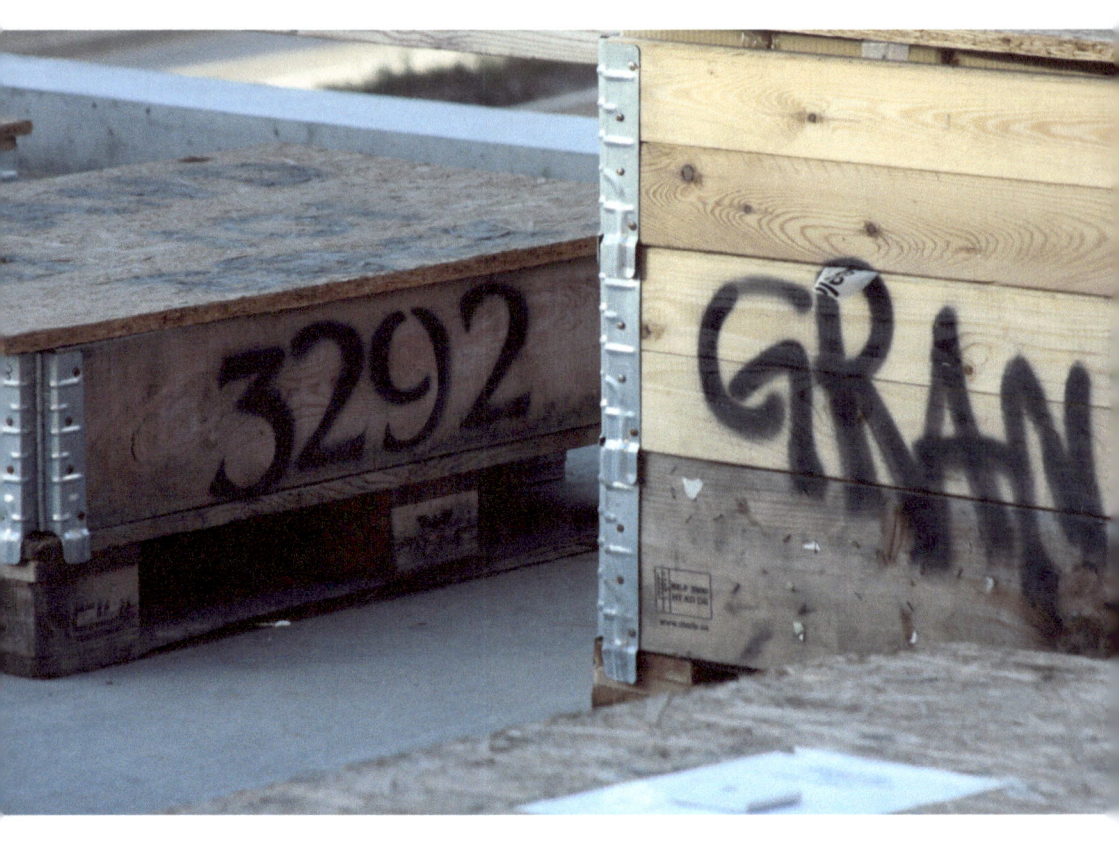

"I need to say one final thing before signing off: The perpetrators of this disaster are still at large. If you see any of these individuals, contact CentralCommand at once."

Han was startled to see his image flash onto the screen with pictures of the five other passengers that had been sick on the flight to Whitehorse.

"I know we will all pull together in the dangerous and difficult days ahead," said Jann. "Every night at six p.m. I and other members of the leadership team will be giving you updates of the situation to keep you informed. Thank you, and God bless America."

The strains of "Hail To The Chief" began as Jann Smyth waved to the camera and was seen shaking hands with a number of junior Senators and Representatives.

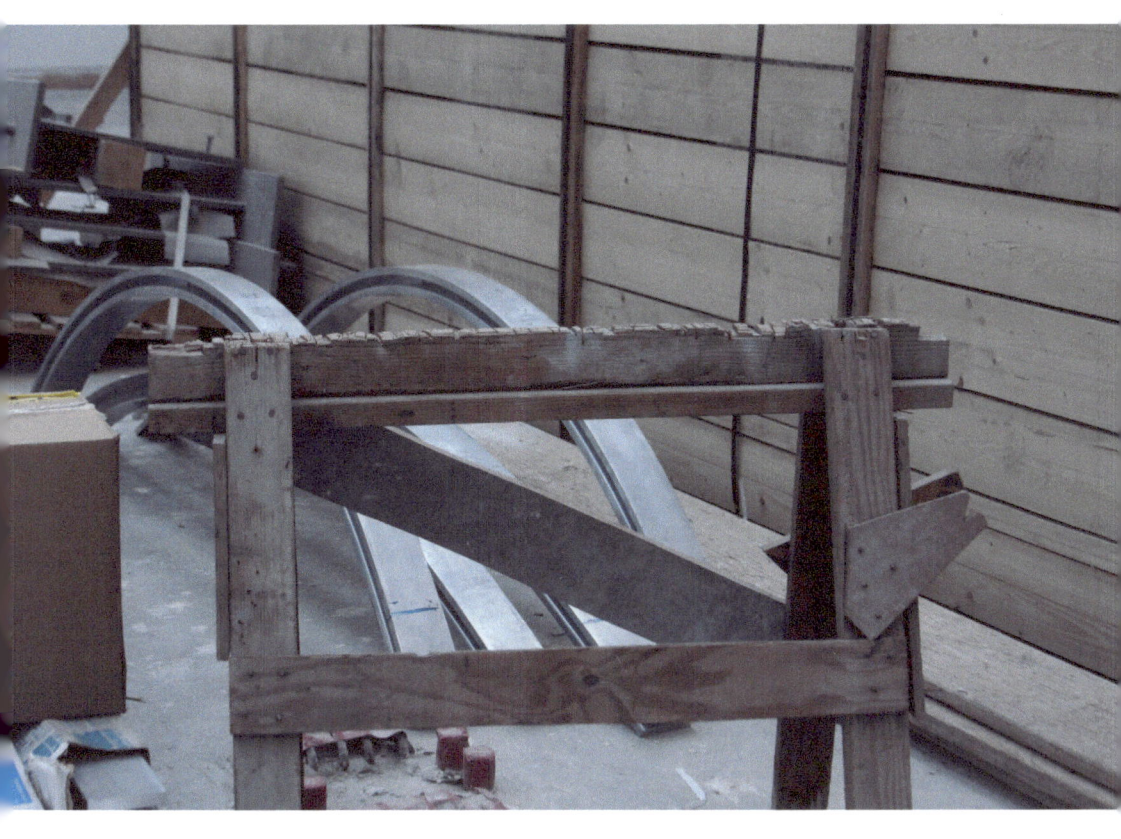

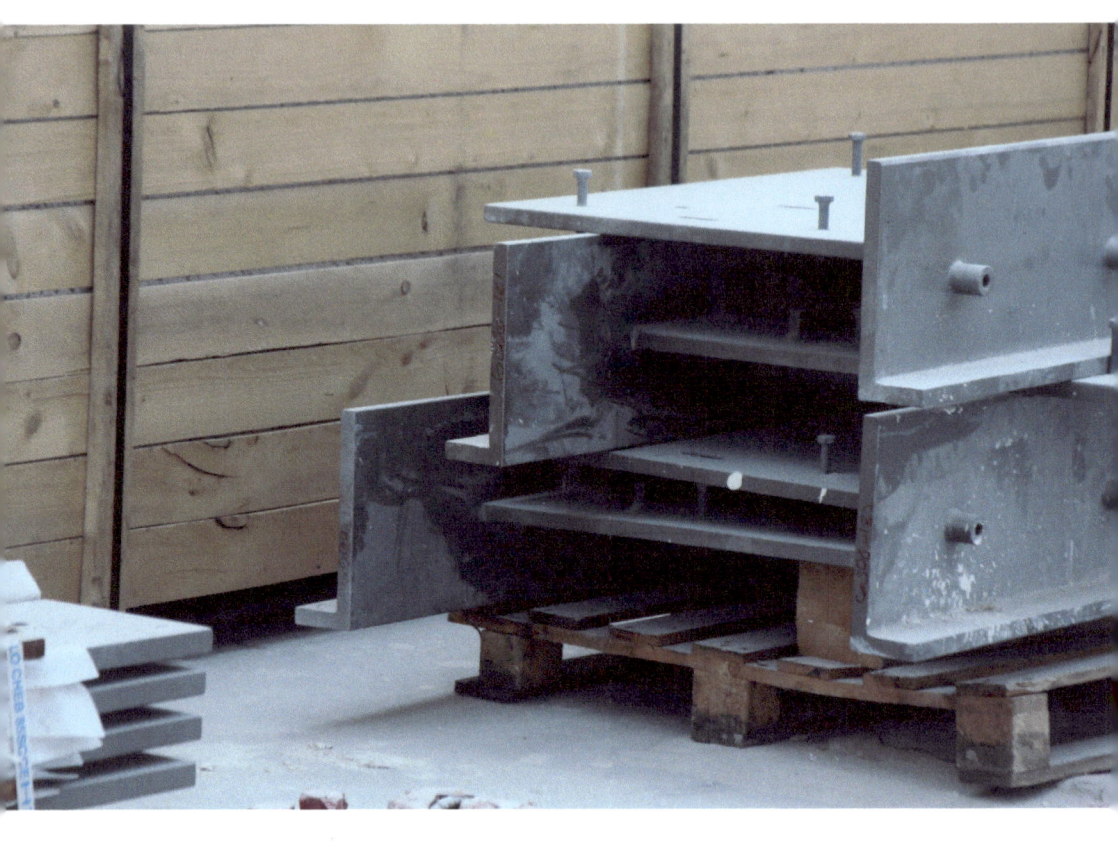

"Take a look at the new leadership core," Cooper said. "Look at all the junior Representatives standing with the President. They probably aren't so junior now."

The screen went dark. A moment later the NewsGraph showed a long directory of information that had just been released on topics related to the President's address.

"With all the panic that will come from this announcement," Jana said, "I'm sorry they distributed your picture, Han. I don't think you'll be able to go out anytime soon."

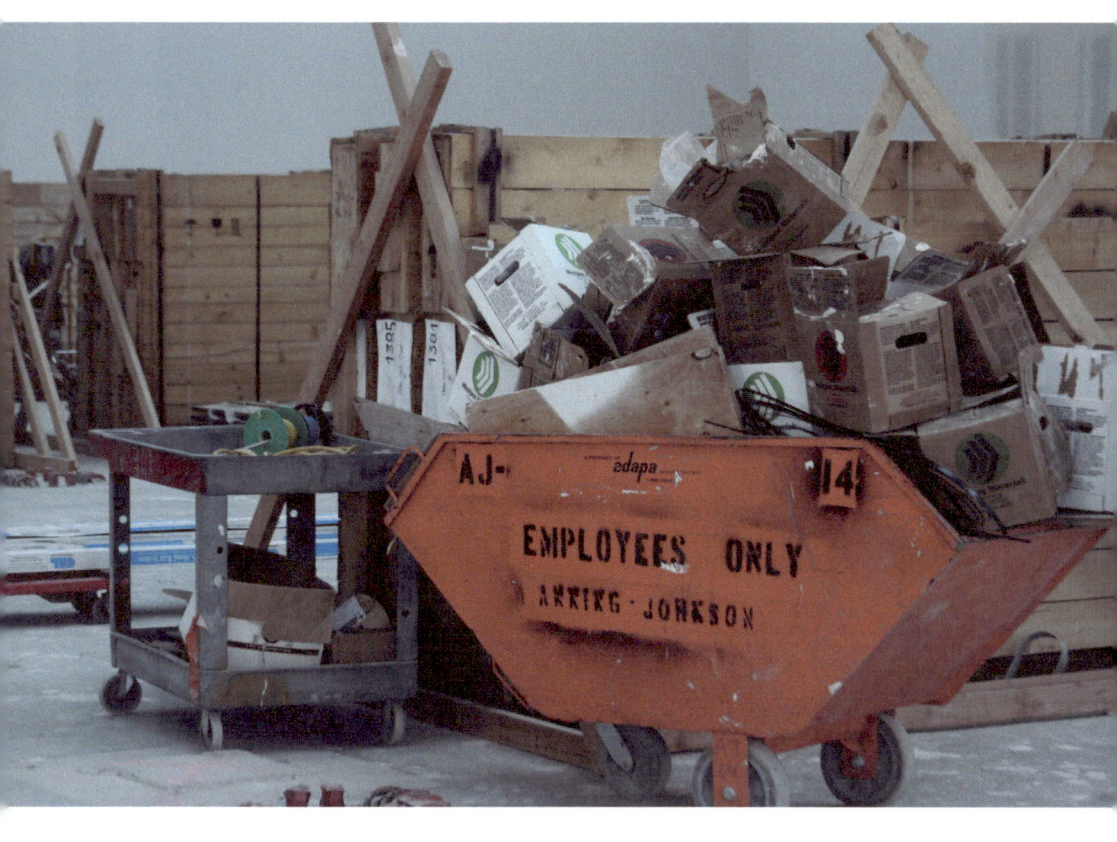

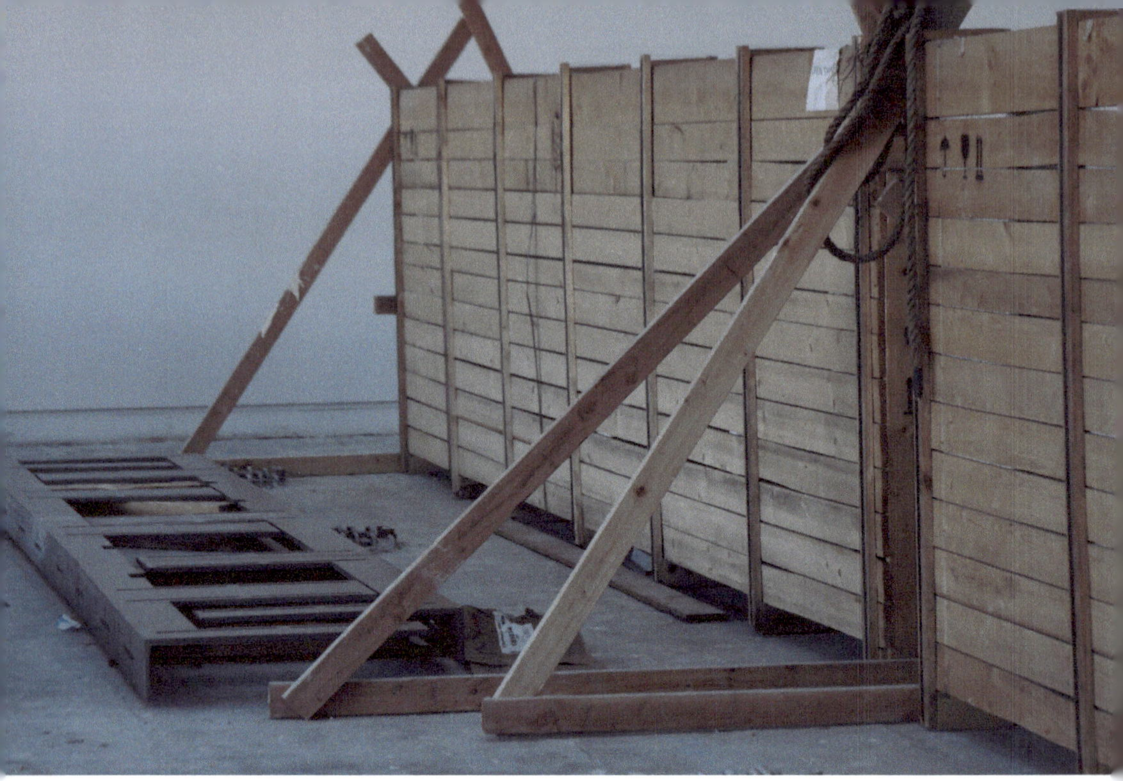

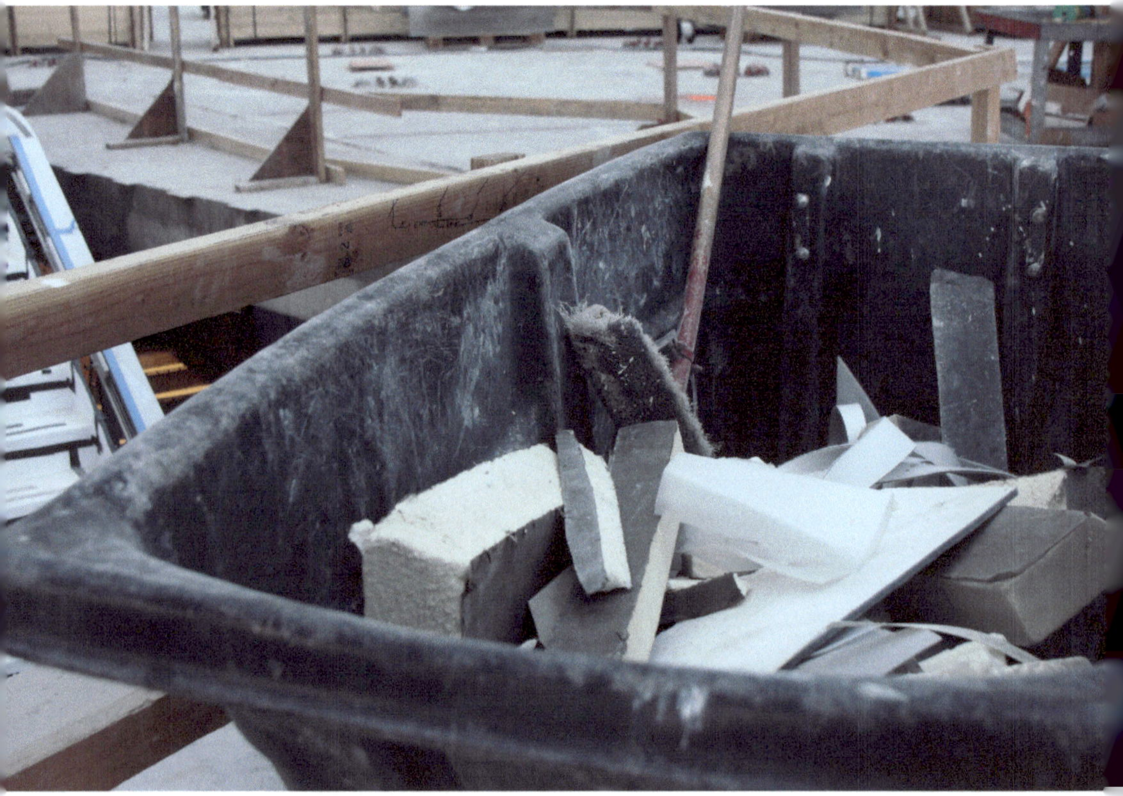

Han was silent. Initially he had thought it would be easy to get home from Whitehorse. Now it looked like it might be impossible.

"Going out is not what I'm worried about," Han said. "I'm wondering which lab is providing the vaccinations."

~~

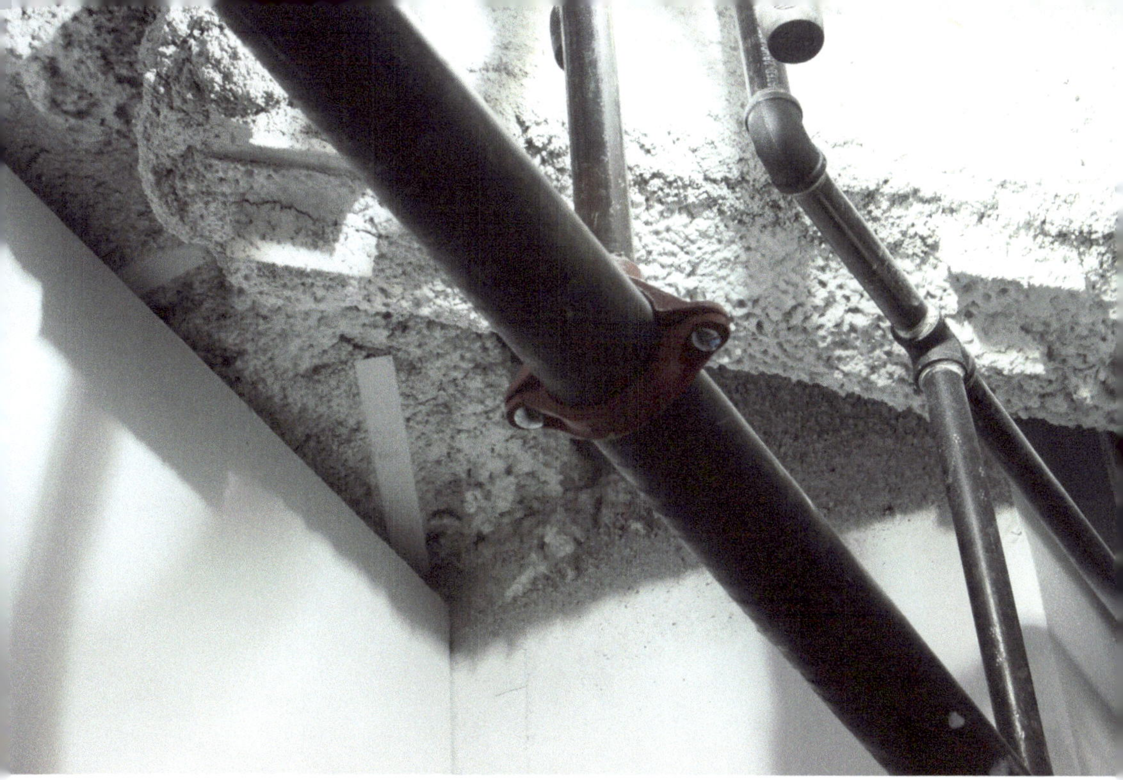

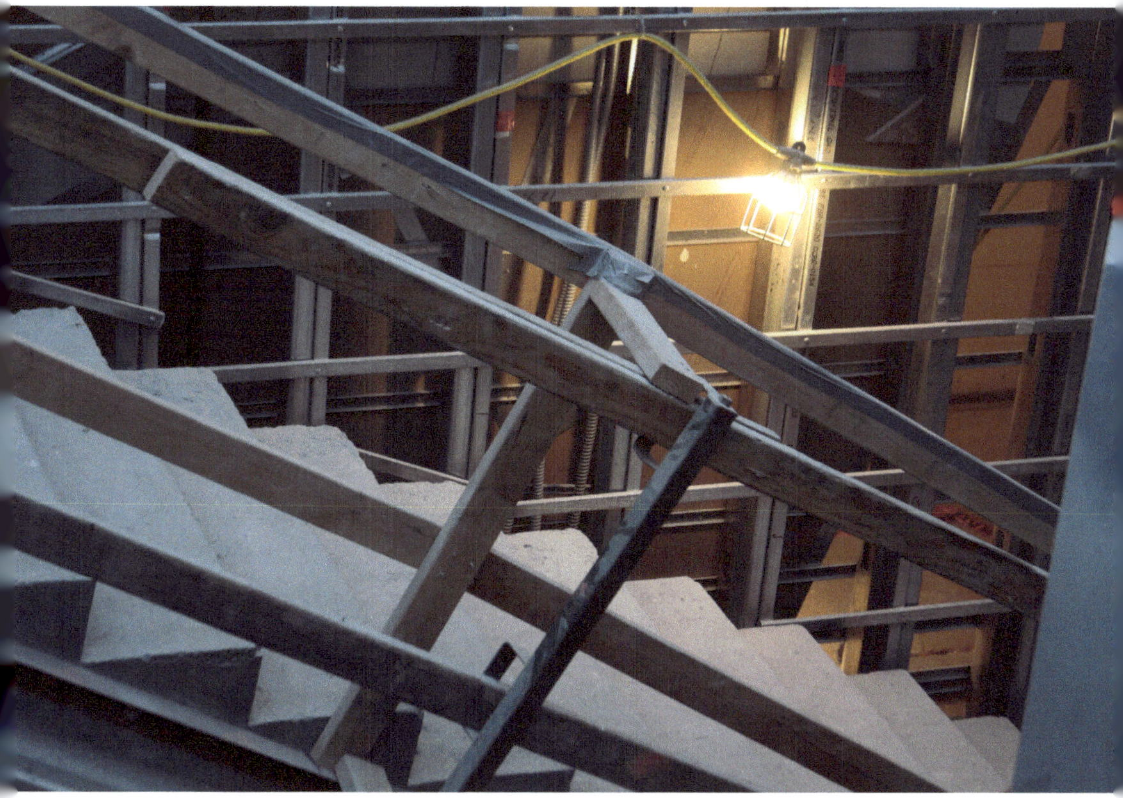

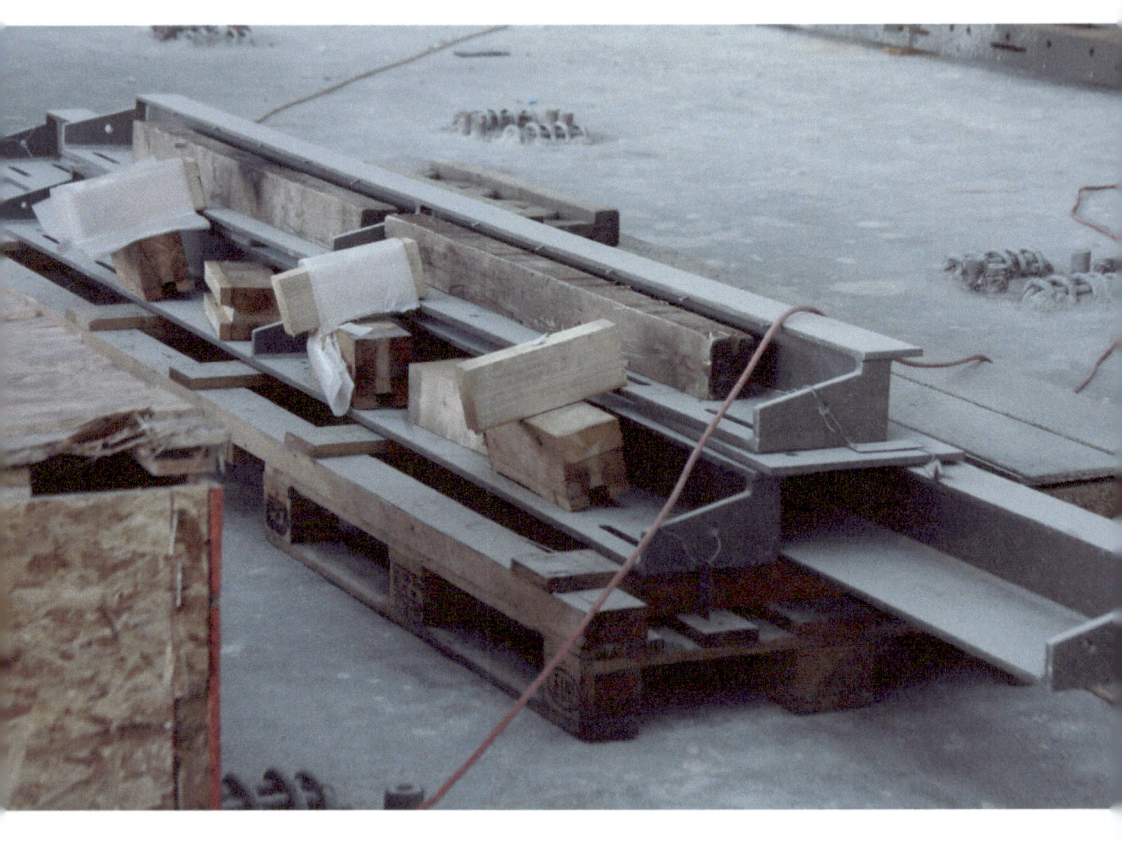

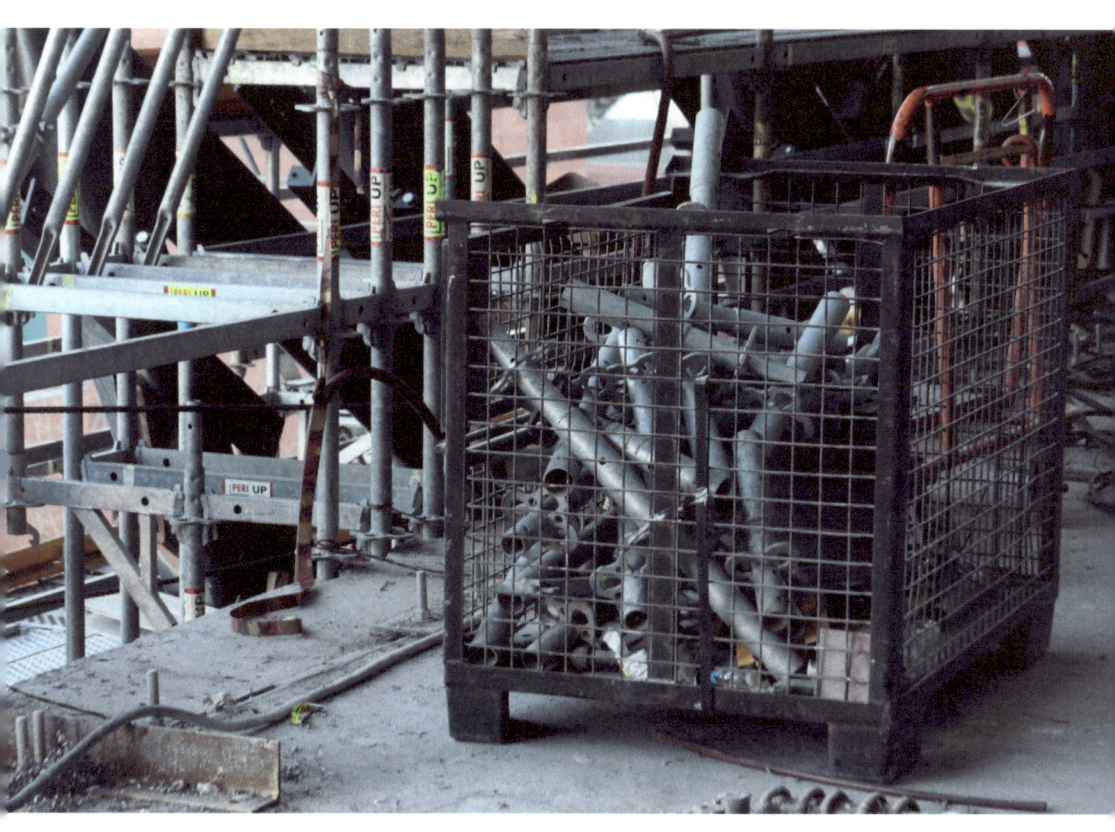

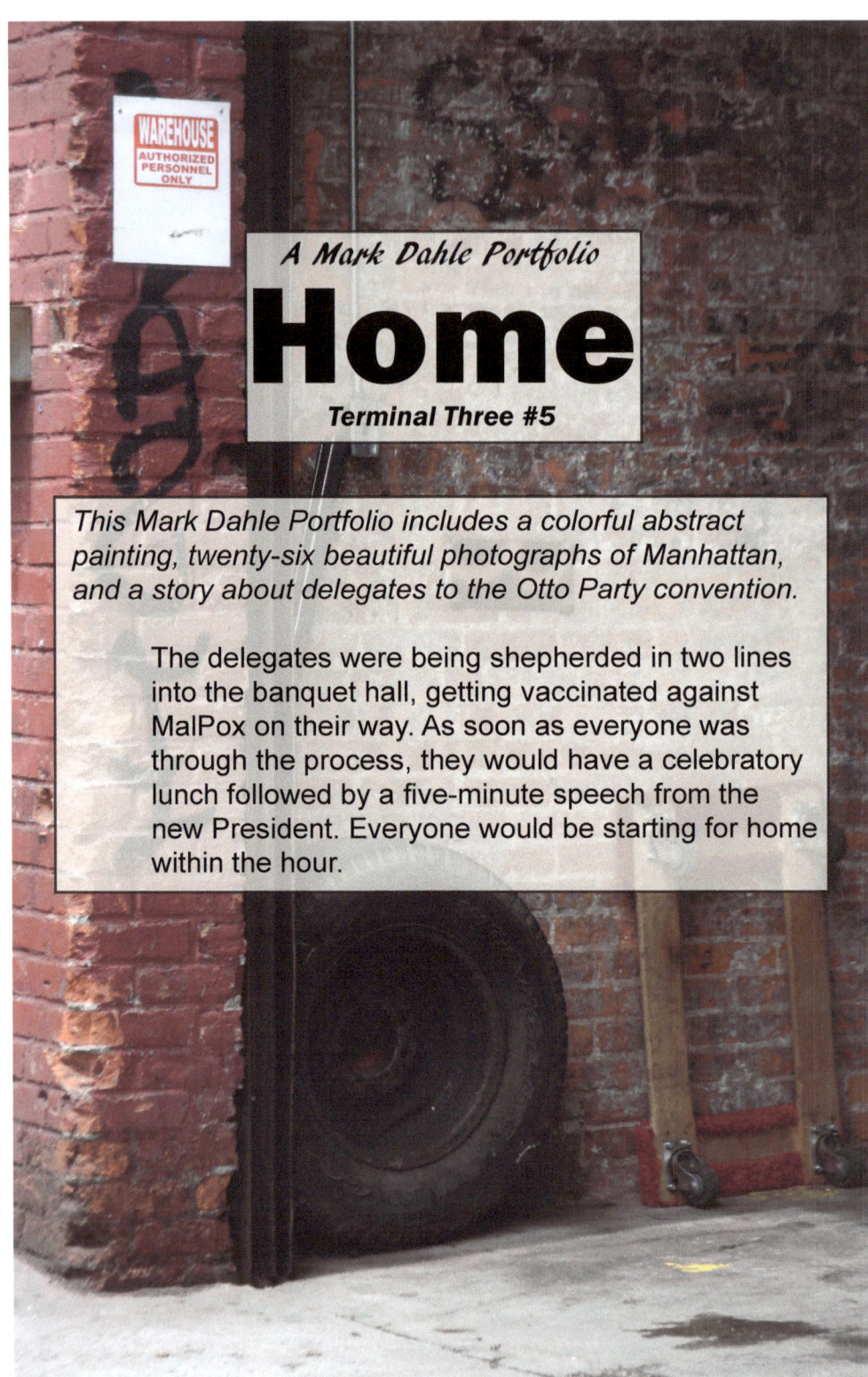

WAREHOUSE
AUTHORIZED
PERSONNEL
ONLY

A Mark Dahle Portfolio

Home

Terminal Three #5

This Mark Dahle Portfolio includes a colorful abstract painting, twenty-six beautiful photographs of Manhattan, and a story about delegates to the Otto Party convention.

The delegates were being shepherded in two lines into the banquet hall, getting vaccinated against MalPox on their way. As soon as everyone was through the process, they would have a celebratory lunch followed by a five-minute speech from the new President. Everyone would be starting for home within the hour.

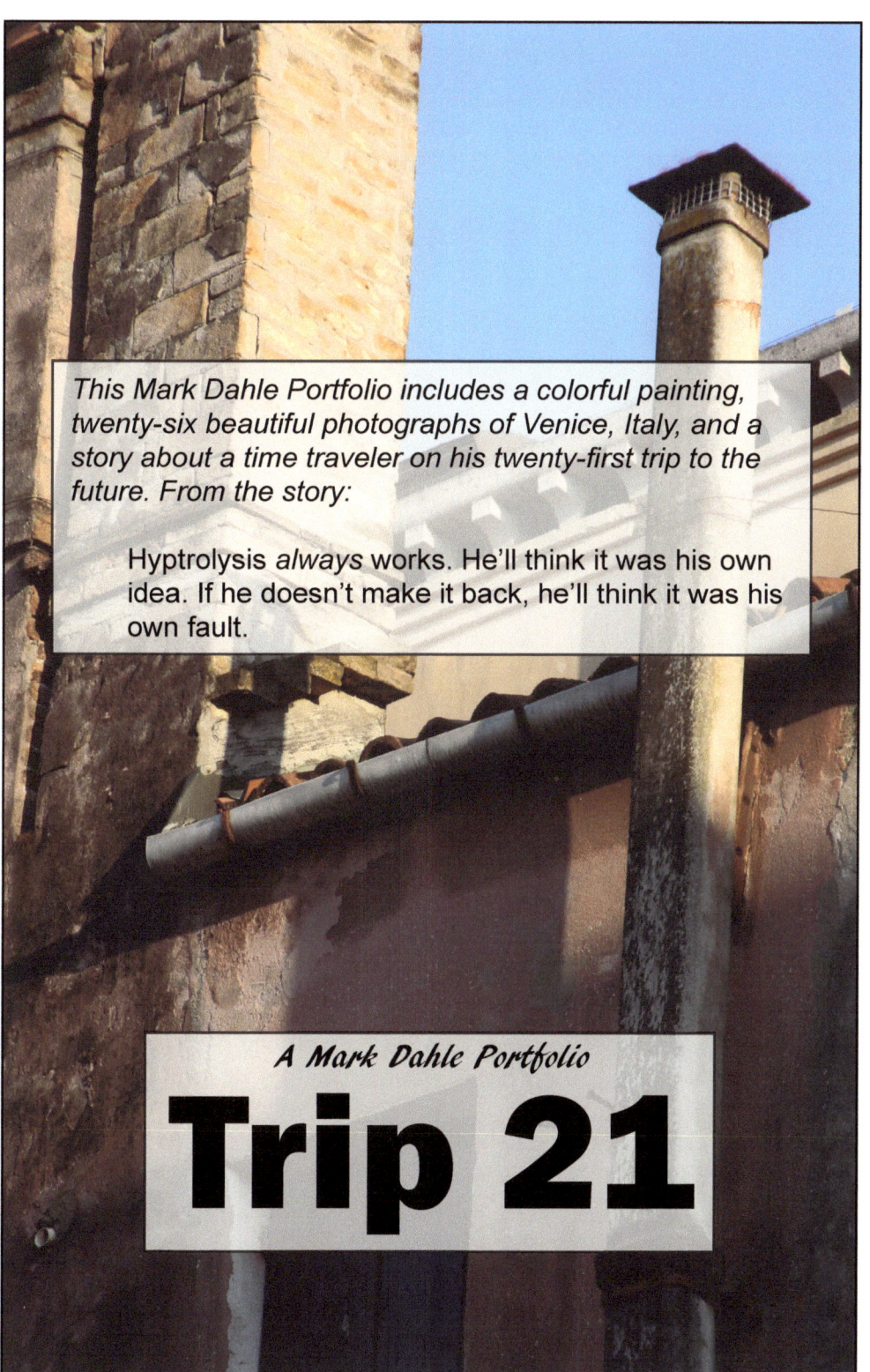

This Mark Dahle Portfolio includes a colorful painting, twenty-six beautiful photographs of Venice, Italy, and a story about a time traveler on his twenty-first trip to the future. From the story:

Hyptrolysis *always* works. He'll think it was his own idea. If he doesn't make it back, he'll think it was his own fault.

A Mark Dahle Portfolio

Trip 21

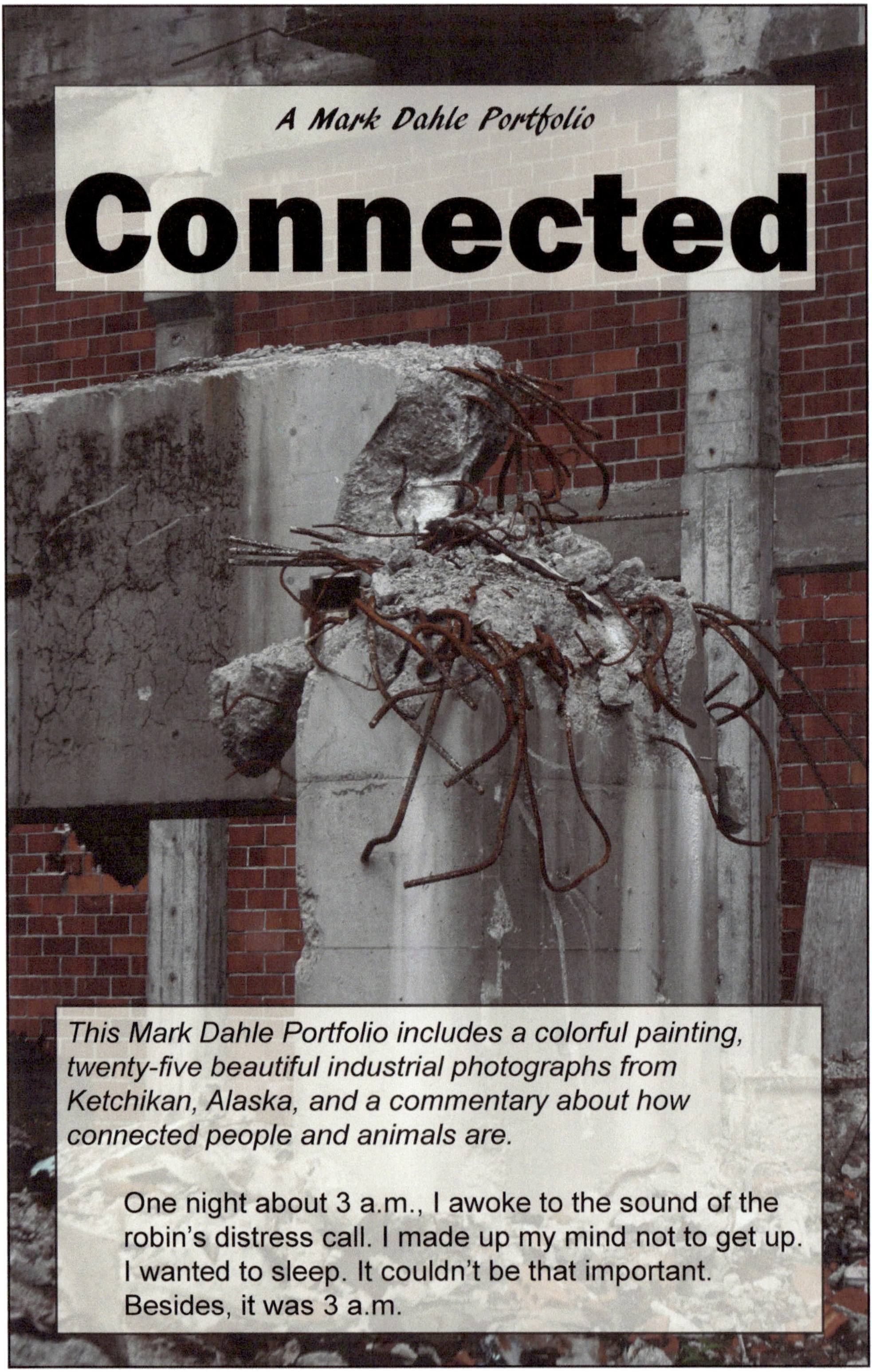

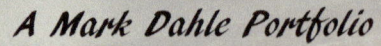

A Mark Dahle Portfolio

Connected

This Mark Dahle Portfolio includes a colorful painting, twenty-five beautiful industrial photographs from Ketchikan, Alaska, and a commentary about how connected people and animals are.

One night about 3 a.m., I awoke to the sound of the robin's distress call. I made up my mind not to get up. I wanted to sleep. It couldn't be that important. Besides, it was 3 a.m.